Titles in the Series

Cerberus

The Chimaera

The Cyclopes

The Monsters of Hercules

Medusa

The Minotaur

The Sirens

The Sphinx

Monsters in Myth

The Sphinx

Pete DiPrimio

Mitchell Lane
PUBLISHERS

P.O. Box 196
Hockessin, Delaware 19707
Visit us on the web: www.mitchelllane.com
Comments? Email us: mitchelllane@mitchelllane.com

Copyright © 2011 by Mitchell Lane Publishers. All rights reserved. No part of this book may be reproduced without written permission from the publisher. Printed and bound in the United States of America.

Printing 1 2 3 4 5 6 7 8 9

Library of Congress Cataloging-in-Publication Data
DiPrimio, Pete.
  The sphinx / by Pete DiPrimio.
      p. cm. — (Monsters in myth)
  Includes bibliographical references and index.
  ISBN 978-1-58415-931-5 (library bound)
  1. Sphinxes (Mythology)—Juvenile literature. I. Title.
  BL820.S66D56 2010
  398.2209182'2—dc22

2010006560

ABOUT THE AUTHOR: Pete DiPrimio is an award-winning sports columnist for the *Fort Wayne* (Indiana) *News-Sentinel* and a longtime freelance feature and travel writer. He is the author of *How'd They Do That in Ancient Rome?* and biographies of Tom Brady, Eli Manning, and Drew Brees for Mitchell Lane Publishers. Pete graduated from Ball State University with honors, earning a Bachelor of Science degree with a minor in history. He lives in Bloomington, Indiana.

AUTHOR'S NOTE: This book retells two ancient stories that involve sphinxes. One is the story of Oedipus, the Sphinx, and the riddle that changed them both forever, based on the version told by Sophocles. The other is the story of the Egyptian prince and future pharaoh Thutmose IV and the Great Sphinx of Giza. These stories are retold using dialogue as an aid to readability. The dialogue is based on the author's research, which is detailed on page 46.

PUBLISHER'S NOTE: This story is based on the author's extensive research, which he believes to be accurate. Documentation of such research is on page 46.
   The Internet sites referenced herein were active as of the publication date. Due to the fleeting nature of some web sites, we cannot guarantee they will all be active when you are reading this book.
   To reflect current usage, we have chosen to use the secular era designations BCE ("before the common era") and CE ("of the common era") instead of the traditional designations BC ("before Christ") and AD (*anno Domini,* "in the year of the Lord").

PLB

TABLE OF CONTENTS

MONSTERS IN MYTH

Chapter One
Riddle Me This 7
For Your Information: Nasty Relatives 13

Chapter Two
Oedipus Finds the Truth 15
For Your Information: A Legend Is Born 21

Chapter Three
From Prince to Pharaoh: Thutmose 23
For Your Information: Harmachis and Horus 29

Chapter Four
Gods, Pharaohs, and the Sphinx 31
For Your Information: What Does It Mean? 37

Chapter Five
Why a Sphinx? 39
For Your Information: Biblical References 43

Chapter Notes 44
Further Reading 45
    Books 45
    Works Consulted 45
    On the Internet 46
Glossary 47
Index 48

The Greeks used images of the Sphinx, which had the head of a woman, the body of a lion, the wings of an eagle, and a serpent's tail, in much of their art.

THE SPHINX

CHAPTER 1
Riddle Me This

The Sphinx paced the rocky ledge outside her mountain cave. She was so angry, flies and mosquitoes buzzed out of her way. The angrier she grew, the faster she paced, and she set a furious tempo as the midday sun blazed from a cloudless sky. Her lion paws dug the outline of her path into the reddish dust that covered the ledge. She flapped her eagle wings and for an instant was tempted to soar into the valley below, down to where the humans lived in a land known as Attica. But that would mean facing an angry Hera, and the Sphinx, as powerful as she was, unbeaten in battle and cunning in confrontations, wanted no part of the goddess' wrath.

The Sphinx had no time for this. She listened to nothing except her own heart. There were lands to explore and food to hunt and she was eager to move on—perhaps fly to the city of Athens near the Gulf of Corinth, or farther to the city of Sparta in the Peloponnese. Instead, she waited for the arrival of Hera, the queen of the gods, who had sent a messenger to say she had a task for her, but refused to say what it was. Hera would meet her outside the Sphinx's cave at noon, the messenger said. As the Sphinx waited and paced, paced and waited, she wished she had eaten the messenger if for no other reason than to calm her rumbling stomach.

The wind began to blow, kicking dust into the Sphinx's green eyes. It blew harder and tossed her long dark hair into a tangled mess. Her face, beautiful enough to steal a man's heart in the blink of an eye, softened with a gentle smile that masked her anger. Hera was coming, and appearances were everything.

CHAPTER 1

Juno, painted by Rembrandt, 1664–1665. Hera was the queen of the Greek gods. The Romans called her Juno.

RIDDLE ME THIS

The Sphinx heard a noise behind her and there was Hera, looking strong and beautiful in a flowing white tunic. She had dark skin, dark eyes, and dark hair. She nodded a greeting to the Sphinx. The Sphinx's smile grew. Hera wasn't fooled. The goddess knew the more the Sphinx smiled, the more dangerous she was.

"I want you to go to Thebes," Hera said, referring to a city on the western edge of Attica. "The people have angered me and I have put a curse on their city. You will carry out the curse."

The Sphinx's smile grew. "What do you want me to do?"

"The Muses have taught you a riddle. You will go to the mountain road that leads into Thebes. You will ask the riddle to whoever passes by. If they answer it, they can go on their way and the curse will be broken. If not, you can do with them what you will."

The Sphinx's smile grew so wide it seemed her face would split in two. She very much enjoyed playing with her food.

"When do you want me to start?" she asked.

"Now," Hera said.

And then she was gone.

Oedipus (EH-dih-pus) stormed up the rocky path. His clothes were torn, his right eye bruised and swollen shut, and another man's blood stained his hands. The fight had been fierce and unexpected and unnecessary. Oedipus was trying to get away—away from his past, from the drunkard at the party telling lies, from a prophecy that could not come true, not if he could help it.

He was the son of Polybus and Merope (MAYR-oh-pee), the king and queen of Corinth. The drunkard had told him he was not their son, and to find the truth Oedipus went to the Oracle at Delphi, the oracle that was never wrong. The oracle told him he would kill his father and marry his mother. He would never do that, but to be safe, he left Corinth and headed east.

At a lonely place in the mountains where three roads meet he had come across a rich, short-tempered, insulting man and his

Chapter 1

servants. The rude man refused to let him pass. Oedipus demanded the way. Rage overcame them and they fought without mercy. Oedipus killed the stranger and then continued on his journey.

Oedipus was tired and battered. His side ached and he wondered if he had broken a rib. The afternoon sun was mercilessly hot. He figured he could find rest and shade in Thebes, the closest city. The path was rough. Rocks chewed his feet into a blistered mess, and his thighs burned from the speed of his pace, but he refused to give in to the pain. He was relieved when he reached the top of Mount Phikion (FY-kee-on), because he could see Thebes about a thousand feet below.

Suddenly, a great creature leaped from a rock and blocked his way. It had the head of a beautiful woman, the body of a lion, a serpent's tail, and eagle wings. It stank like spoiled meat. Oedipus pretended not to notice.

"Who goes there?" the creature asked.

"I am Oedipus of Corinth. Why are you blocking my path?"

"Hera has cursed Thebes," the creature said. "No one can pass unless they answer my riddle."

Oedipus eyed the creature. He could see her powerful muscles rippling under her tawny hide, her daggerlike claws and sharp teeth. He saw cold cruelty in her green eyes. An ordinary man would have turned back, but Oedipus was not ordinary.

"What is your riddle?"

The Sphinx came close enough to hug, close enough to slug. The stench was overpowering, and it was all Oedipus could do not to get sick to his stomach.

"What goes on four legs at dawn, two legs in the day, and three legs in the evening?" she asked smugly. She gazed hungrily at him, and Oedipus knew she saw him as just another meal.

"No one has ever gotten it right," she said. She shoved aside a large boulder and exposed a shallow grave filled with human bones,

RIDDLE ME THIS

Oedipus and the Sphinx, by Gustave Moreau, 1864. Oedipus would have to solve a riddle to survive. If he answered wrong, the Sphinx would kill him and eat him.

CHAPTER 1

the bones of those who had failed to solve the riddle. "I can't tell you how many good meals that has meant for me."

Oedipus looked down at Thebes. He watched people move on the streets far below and wondered if he'd ever get to join them.

"It's a good riddle," he said, stalling for time. "Where did you learn it?"

"From the Muses," the Sphinx said. The Muses were nine goddess sisters who inspired artists, poets, philosophers, and musicians. "What's your answer?"

From the mountain Oedipus watched the Thebans—the young, the middle-aged, the old. And then the answer hit him like a thunderbolt from Zeus.

"The answer is man," he said softly. "As a child it crawls on all fours. As an adult it walks upright on two legs. As an old person it needs a staff to walk, and moves as if it had three legs."

The Sphinx listened without blinking, breathing, or moving. Oedipus saw anger building in her eyes like a great storm. And then she smiled.

"Did you hear me?" he asked. "The answer is man."

The Sphinx's breath came out in explosive hisses, each louder than the one before. Her face flushed red. A vein bulged from her forehead as if ready to burst. Her smile grew.

"I guess you won't be eating so well tonight," Oedipus said.

The Sphinx roared loud enough to wake the dead. She roared again and the echoes bounced off the mountains so that the Thebans looked up in wonder. The Sphinx smashed a paw into the boulder, and pieces of rock cut Oedipus's face. And then she jumped, soaring into the air for a second before folding her wings and diving to the rocks below. Her great body crashed, and Oedipus knew she could not have survived the impact.

After a long pause, Oedipus headed toward Thebes and his destiny.[1,2]

F.Y.I.
For Your Information

Nasty Relatives

The Greek Sphinx was the daughter of two other mythical creatures—Typhon and Echidna.

According to some descriptions, Typhon had a hundred dragon heads, each with fangs loaded with poison and eyes that shot fire. Snakes grew from his winged body. As Zeus, the king of the gods, discovered, it was unwise to anger Typhon. At the urging of his mother, Gaia (known as Mother Earth), Typhon drove all the gods from Mount Olympus and into Egypt. That way Gaia could rule the earth. Zeus, protecting his godly rights, fought with Typhon, who took Zeus's lightning bolts. Typhon won. He carried Zeus to his cave and tore the ligaments out of Zeus's arms and legs so that the god could not move.

Typhon left Zeus in that state, and the gods Pan and Hermes found him. Hermes put Zeus back together. Vowing revenge, Zeus prepared for a rematch. When they met again, Zeus won, and he buried Typhon under Mount Etna (a volcano on the Italian island of Sicily). Legend says Typhon causes Mount Etna to erupt. He is also believed to be the cause of dangerous winds. The storm "typhoon" is named after him.

Echidna, called the Mother of all Monsters, had the head and upper body of a beautiful nymph and the lower body of a snake. She had speckled skin and liked to eat raw flesh. She and Typhon had monstrous children: the Chimaera (a fire-breathing beast with three heads: a lion at the front, a goat in the middle, and a snake or dragon for a tail), the Hydra (a large snake with several heads), the Nemean Lion (a huge lion with skin no arrow or spear could pierce), Orthus (a two-headed dog), Cerberus (a three-headed dog who guarded the Underworld), and the cunning Sphinx. (According to some accounts, the Sphinx was the daughter of Orthus and the Chimaera.)

The Chimaera

After defeating Typhon, Zeus allowed Echidna and her children to live as challenges to future heroes. Echidna was eventually killed by Argus, the hundred-eyed giant.

Oedipus and the Sphinx, painted by Jean-Auguste-Dominique Ingres in 1808. For ridding Thebes of Hera's curse, Oedipus would win the hand of Queen Jocasta.

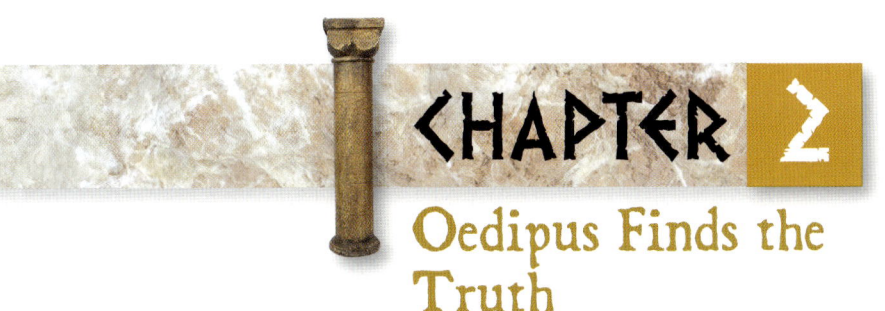

CHAPTER 2
Oedipus Finds the Truth

Pounding at the door forced Jocasta out of bed. Cheers from an outside celebration over the naming of the new king roared through the palace window. She passed a wooden table littered with an uneaten dinner next to an uneaten lunch and breakfast.

"He's here, your majesty," a servant said from behind the door.

"Leave me alone," she said. "Tell him to go away."

"The people have decided," the servant said. He had been with the queen long enough to know what she said wasn't always what she meant. "You don't have a choice."

"There's always a choice," she replied. After a moment, she began dressing in black, the only color she would wear, even though the official period of mourning her dead husband Laius was long over. She dressed slowly. It was nearly an hour before she reached the reception room and saw a handsome young man waving to the crowd from a window. He turned to her and smiled. He had long dark hair, a strong chin, and kind blue eyes. He reminded her of Laius.

"What is your name?" the queen asked.

"I am Oedipus," he said. "I am the son of Polybus and Merope, the king and queen of Corinth."

The queen paused. She knew that *Oedipus* meant "swollen foot."

"That is an unusual name," she said.

"My parents named me that because, as a boy, my feet and ankles were swollen."

Jocasta gasped and remembered the time she had sworn to forget, when a newborn was torn from her arms, when Laius pinned

CHAPTER 2

the baby's feet together to gut-wrenching cries and ordered her to never speak of the child again. Her husband had done the right thing, she'd told herself until she stopped crying. In time, she'd almost believed it.

"You are the man who saved us from the Sphinx," she said softly.

Oedipus nodded. Her servant approached them. "He's the man you have to marry. Are you ready?"

Jocasta listened to the cheering crowd. "So I am the reward."

"No," Oedipus said. "The city is."

Years later, Oedipus stood before his throne, eyes hard, voice sharp.

"We will find the real murderer and end this curse," he said.

Jocasta sat on the edge of her throne, hands folded on her lap as if in prayer. "Let it go," she said with a trembling voice.

He glared at the woman who had given him two daughters and two sons.

"Crops have died. Women can't have children. You know what the oracle has said. The curse ends when the murderer of Laius is found and either exiled or killed. You've heard the lies and know they will spread and what the people will think and do. How can I let it go?"

"You have to," Jocasta said.

Oracles could not be ignored. They were priests or priestesses who, through the power of the gods, saw the future in the movement of birds, the rustling of leaves, or the analyzing of dreams. Greeks used them to help them make important decisions. The most famous oracles were those of Apollo at the city of Delphi and Zeus at the city of Dodona.

Oedipus took down a bronze sword hanging on a stone wall. He was tired of the lies and confusion and, most of all, a growing fear deep in the pit of his stomach. First, there was Jocasta's brother,

OEDIPUS FINDS THE TRUTH

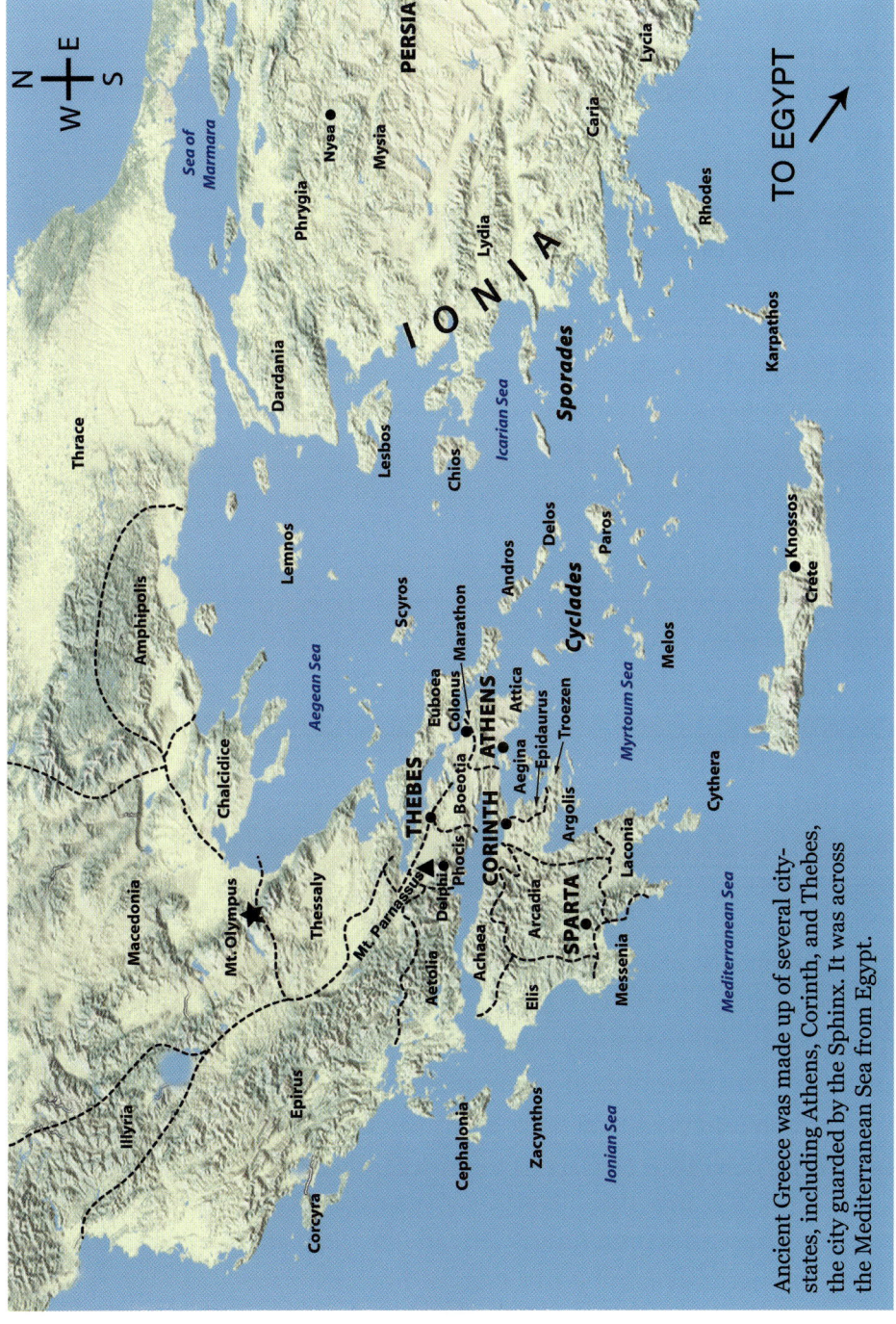

Ancient Greece was made up of several city-states, including Athens, Corinth, and Thebes, the city guarded by the Sphinx. It was across the Mediterranean Sea from Egypt.

CHAPTER 2

Creon, revealing what the Oracle at Delphi had said about ending the curse. Then there was the blind prophet, Teiresias, accusing Oedipus of being the killer. That was impossible. He'd never met Laius.

And yet ...

Jocasta had said her husband had been killed at a place where three roads met. Oedipus remembered his fight with a wealthy stranger at a place like that many years before. But that man had been rude and acted nothing like a king. One of the man's servants had survived the attack and still lived outside of Thebes. Oedipus sent soldiers to bring him to the palace so that they would all know the truth.

Then there was the prophecy that Oedipus would kill his father and marry his mother. That was crazy. His parents were Polybus and Merope. Hadn't a messenger just arrived saying Polybus had died and the people of Corinth wanted him, because he was Polybus's son, to be their new king?

Oedipus wouldn't go there because Merope was still alive and the prophecy made him feel uneasy around her. But the messenger had said that Oedipus shouldn't worry because he was an adopted son, that Polybus and Merope were not his real parents. That was another lie, of course. The messenger was old and foolish. When the messenger insisted that he had once been a shepherd and had found Oedipus as a baby abandoned on a mountain and had taken him to Polybus and Merope, Oedipus had lost his temper. He yelled and banged his fist on tables and accused the messenger of lying. The messenger said that there was a servant who could prove his story because that servant had abandoned the baby on the mountain. It was the same servant who was on his way to the palace. Oedipus ordered everyone to leave so that he could think.

"Oedipus," Jocasta said softly, "please don't do this."

She cried into her hands. In all the years they'd known each other, he had never seen her cry.

OEDIPUS FINDS THE TRUTH

"Go rest," he said, touching her hair. "I'll take care of this."

Jocasta ran from the room. Oedipus went to a window and looked out over the city he had ruled wisely and well for so long. He had done the right things all his life. He knew he was a good person and that all of this was wrong, that there was a simple explanation and that they would all laugh when the truth came out.

So why was he so afraid?

Soldiers led an old man into the room. The man had long white hair and walked with a cane. He coughed after every breath.

"Do you know why you're here?" Oedipus asked.

The old man clutched his cane. "The whole city knows."

Oedipus lifted his sword, running a finger over the blade to feel its sharpness. "I want the truth. If you lie, it will be your last."

"My life has been a lie since I took you into the mountains to die," the old man said. "I lied that I had killed you because I could not kill a baby. I lied when you returned to Thebes as a hero for answering the riddle. I lied when I watched you marry your mother and have children with her. Now you force me to tell the truth and if you kill me for it, well, I am old and ready for the Underworld."

Oedipus trembled at the words. He saw the truth in the old man's eyes, felt it in his own heart, realized the horrible things he had done. He dropped the sword and ran from the room, ran to their bedroom to hear the truth from Jocasta's lips. The door was locked so he smashed it open with his shoulder. Jocasta was there, hanging by a rope around her neck, as dead as his hopes for a happy life. He took two pins from her clothes and gouged out his eyes so that he'd never have to look at himself again. He would leave the city and never return. He yelled for Creon, who would be the new king. Oedipus asked only to hug his children one last time because they were the only good things to come from this tragedy.

"Where will you go?" Creon asked.

"To die," Oedipus said.

CHAPTER 2

Oedipus at Colonus, painted in 1798 by Fulchran-Jean Harriet. The suffering of Oedipus did not stop with his exile. His sons fought each other to the death, and his daughter Antigone died when King Creon punished her for burying one of them.

Oedipus wandered blindly through the country with his daughter Antigone (an-TIH-guh-nee) as his guide. Theseus, king of Athens, gave him protection, and he finally died in the city of Colonus.[1]

The myth of the Sphinx of Thebes might have started in Egypt and moved to Greece. Ancient Greeks and Egyptians had a lot of contact with each other. Two of their greatest cities, Athens in Greece and Alexandria in Egypt, were separated only by the Mediterranean Sea. Sphinxes were popular in Greek art. They appear on Greek vases and on the tombs of young men.

For the Greeks, the Sphinx represented destruction and bad luck. The Egyptians saw the Sphinx as a guardian, a god, and a gatekeeper to a better world.

A Legend Is Born

The Sphinx myth started in Egypt at least five thousand years ago. The name *Sphinx* evolved from the Egyptian word *Shesep-ankh*, which means "living image." As the years passed, it changed to come from the Greek word *sphingo*, which means "to strangle," or from the Greek word *sphingein*, which means "to bind tight." Either way, it wasn't much fun to run into a Greek sphinx because it would strangle and then eat its victims.[2]

The Egyptian sphinx wasn't as violent as the Greek sphinx. Called an andro-sphinx (man-sphinx), it was a male with the head of a king and the body of a lion. Because lions symbolized guardians for ancient Egyptians, sphinx statues were used as protectors or guardians over temples and sacred buildings. Egyptian criosphinxes (ram-sphinxes) had the head of a ram, which symbolized the power of the Egyptian god Amun, a powerful leader like the Greek god Zeus. Hieracosphinxes (hawk-sphinxes) had the head of a hawk. Male gods were usually bulls, rams, falcons, or lions. Female gods were cows, vultures, cobras, and lionesses.[3]

Ancient sphinx statues were made from native rock in the desert sands at Giza, a famous Egyptian site west of Cairo and the Nile River. That's the location of the Great Sphinx statue and the Great Pyramids.

The sphinx legend eventually moved into Mesopotamia, which is now called the Middle East. As it moved, wings were added. In Crete, a small island in the Mediterranean Sea near Greece, winged sphinxes began appearing on artifacts during the sixteenth century BCE. About 100 years later, Greek art showed the sphinx with the head of a woman and the winged body of a lion, usually sitting down. By the seventh century BCE, sphinx images were appearing on Greek friezes (a decorative band on the upper part of a wall in a room) and vases. The Greeks turned the sphinx into a female spirit called an incubus.

The tomb of Pharaoh Thutmose IV is located in the Valley of the Kings. Although it was robbed in antiquity, these valuable objects remained inside it. The mummy of Thutmose was relocated to the tomb of his father, Amenhotep II, sometime after.

THE SPHINX

CHAPTER 3
From Prince to Pharaoh: Thutmose

Prince Thutmose scanned the hot desert with cool eyes. His brothers—he had so many it was hard to keep track of them all—wanted to destroy him. No problem. His father, the king of Egypt (Pharaoh Amenhotep II), wasn't sure if he was the man to become king when the time came, in part because Amenhotep had an older son who was first in line to the throne. Thutmose had learned to live with that. He was confident, powerful, and patient, and he could command others as easily as taking a breath. That he was not yet twenty was a problem for the old, but not for him. He would handle his brothers and prove himself to his father—but those were tasks for another day. What mattered now was the hunt. Antelope and gazelles were out there—fast and fit and elusive. So were lions, great beasts as powerful as any in Egypt. Only a great hunter could bring one down in these conditions. Thutmose very much wanted to be great.

All the Egyptian royalty had gathered at Heliopolis (hee-lee-AH-puh-lis), whose name in Greek means "city of the sun," just northwest of the famous city of Cairo. It was near the great Nile River, the longest river in the world. They were at Heliopolis to celebrate the festival of Re, the Egyptian sun god and creator god. Thutmose couldn't stand all the ceremony and gossip and arguing, so he slipped away when no one was looking. He brought two servants with him—his father had ordered him not to go anywhere alone. *For your protection*, the father had said. *To spy on me*, the son whispered. His father did not yet trust him, still treated him like a boy when he was really a man. He would slip away from the servants later.

Thutmose liked to hunt alone, especially in the desert. When treated with respect, the desert was beautiful. Those who were smart

CHAPTER 3

The Nile River has been vital to the Egyptian people since ancient times. Beyond the banks of the river stretches the desert.

and knew their limitations—and knew what the desert would allow them to do—were fine. For those who made stupid mistakes, the desert could be as ruthless as a hungry lion.

Thutmose was a great warrior. He never missed as an archer. He could draw his bow and fire arrows so fast it was as if he had four arms. He could drive chariots as well as anyone in Egypt, and because he was royalty he had the best and fastest horses. He loved the way the wind blew his long dark hair as he pushed his horses to the limit. He wanted to push now, so he took a chariot and headed beyond the green cultivated earth near the Nile and into the harsh red desert.

FROM PRINCE TO PHARAOH: THUTMOSE

Thutmose and his servants left before dawn to beat the brutal heat of the desert sun. They would try to finish hunting before noon, when it would be too hot for anything but resting in the shade.

Eventually they reached an oasis of palm trees and water. Thutmose told his servants to wait for him there. They readily complied. Only Thutmose liked to hunt in these conditions.

He traveled north, most of the time close enough to the Nile to see it. He found a few antelope tracks, but he didn't see the animals that made them. He knew it was getting time to rest and pray to the great god Harmachis (HAR-mah-kis), the god of the rising sun. The god's temple was at Giza, a sacred area and the place where the Great Pyramids towered over the desert like mountains.[1]

There were three pyramids built to honor the pharaohs Khufu (also known as Cheops), Khafre (or Chephren), and Menkaure (or Mykerinos). The pyramids had stood for more than 1,200 years, surviving the harsh sun and blasting winds. They were the largest buildings ever constructed, and Thutmose never tired of the sight.[2,3]

What really struck him was the carved stone head and neck looming out of the sand perhaps twenty feet high. It was the Great Sphinx. Some said it was carved to look like Khafre. Others said it represented Harmachis. It didn't matter. There was shade under the statue. The heat had sapped Thutmose's strength. He would pray and rest, and then get his servants and return to the festival and whatever plots his brothers had cooked up while he was gone.

Thutmose quickly fell asleep, but he awoke to the sound of a voice. It was deep and loud and shook the sand like an earthquake. He realized it was coming from the Great Sphinx, but it was no longer a statue. It was alive, a creature—it was the god Harmachis himself, and Thutmose suddenly felt very afraid.

"Do not fear," the voice said. "I am here to ask for your help."

Thutmose rose to his feet. He tried to keep the trembling out of his voice. "How can I help you? I am just a man. You are a god."

CHAPTER 3

"I am a god, but I am no match for the desert wind and sand," the voice said. "For centuries I have been buried like this. I long to have the sun warm my body. I want to show the world what I really look like. I want to be free."

"I understand," Thutmose said. He used his right hand to shade his eyes from the sun so that he could get a better look at the creature. The stone had taken on the appearance of skin. The eyes were warm and kind. "What do you want me to do?"

"I want you to free me from this prison. I want you to clear away the sand and let me be as I was meant to be. If you do this, I will see to it that you will be pharaoh. And not just a pharaoh, but a great one who will be remembered until the end of time."

"There are some who do not want me to be pharaoh," Thutmose said. "They will do everything they can to convince my father I am not worthy. They might even try to get rid of me by setting up an accident."

"Like hunting alone in the desert?" the voice asked.

Thutmose couldn't help smiling. "Something like that."

"If you do what I ask they won't be able to hurt you," the voice said. "The entire kingdom of Egypt will be yours. You will have riches and power and fame. You will live a long and happy life. When you need wisdom, I will give it. When you need good luck, I will provide it."

The voice paused.

"Will you help me?"

"Of course I will help you," Thutmose said.

And then the sand shook and Thutmose fell and the world went black. When he awoke he remembered all that had happened. Was it a dream? Was it real? It didn't matter. He would keep his promise. He would go back to his father and tell him the Great Sphinx had to be cleared of sand. He would beg, argue, convince. Nothing would stop him. He ran to his chariot and rode hard back to the oasis. His

FROM PRINCE TO PHARAOH: THUTMOSE

Egypt is full of ancient treasures, from the Sphinx and Great Pyramids of Giza to the sacred tombs in the Valley of the Kings. Thebes (Luxor) is not to be confused with Thebes in Greece. The Suez Canal was not built until 1869.

CHAPTER 3

The Eye of Horus (also Eye of Re) represents the sun god who ruled ancient Egypt. Egyptians believed the pharaohs were the human form of Horus.

servants jumped up when they heard him coming. They could tell something had happened.

"Great Prince, what is wrong?" one of the servants asked.

"Nothing," the prince said. "Everything is perfect."

And so it was. Amenhotep eventually named Thutmose his heir to the throne. Thutmose became a great pharaoh, ruling from 1401 to 1391 BCE. He is most famous for restoring the Great Sphinx and placing a 15-ton carved granite slab known as the Dream Stele between the Sphinx's paws. It tells the story of Thutmose's dream. He would also crush some minor uprisings and sign a peace treaty with the neighboring Mitanni Empire in what is now Syria.

All thanks to the Sphinx and its promise.

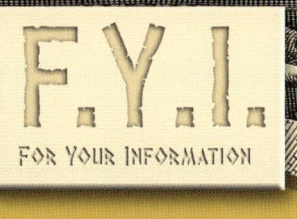

Harmachis and Horus

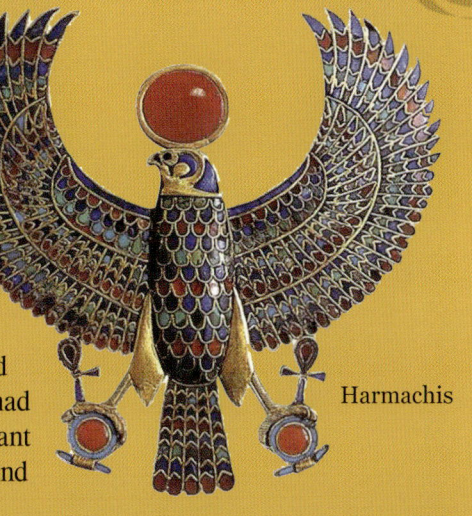

Harmachis

The falcon god Horus was the son of Osiris, the god of nature who controlled the Nile River, which was the lifeblood of Egypt. Osiris once ruled Egypt with help from his wife and sister, Isis. Osiris had a jealous brother, Seth, who killed Osiris, cut him into pieces, and scattered the parts all over the desert. Isis gathered all the parts and brought Osiris back to life, but he had had enough of being in charge. He didn't want to mess with Seth, so he retired and became lord of the underworld.

Horus wasn't about to let Seth get away with what he had done to his father. He challenged Seth for control of Egypt. They met in an epic battle. Horus lost an eye. Seth was castrated. The earth god, Geb, ruled that Horus was the winner and would be king of Egypt for all time. However, he would rule through human bodies. In other words, each pharaoh was said to be the human form of Horus. When a pharaoh died, he joined Osiris in the afterlife, and the next pharaoh became the human form of Horus all over again.

Seth

The Egyptians gave Horus different names depending on his different forms, such as Harpokrates (Horus the child), which referred to his birth, and Haroeris (Horus the elder), which referred to when he battled Seth.[4]

Harmachis (Horus of the Two Horizons) refers to his form as the god of the rising sun, which is the role of the Egyptian Sphinx (head of a pharaoh, body of a lion). The two horizons represent sunrise and sunset.

Noon, which is midway between sunrise and sunset, was when Harmachis's power was at its strongest. It was the perfect time for the encounter between the god and the Egyptian prince Thutmose.[5]

Egyptians believed that Osiris, shown in an ancient hieroglyph, was the god of nature who governed the Nile River and all of Egypt.

CHAPTER 4
Gods, Pharaohs, and the Sphinx

Egypt started as separate North and South kingdoms, called Lower Egypt in the north and Upper Egypt in the south. Egyptian legend says a god-king named Menes, the king of Upper Egypt, conquered Lower Egypt and built the white-walled capital of Memphis around 3000 BCE.

Because Egypt was surrounded by desert and the Mediterranean Sea, it grew without being bothered by its warlike neighbors. It developed a religion of fierce gods and a religion-centered government that produced some of the greatest architectural wonders of the ancient world.

Early on, local chiefs claimed to have mystical powers because they were related to local gods. They often lived in those gods' temples, so everyone knew who had the power and why. Animals seemed especially powerful to the early Egyptians, which is why they used animals to represent their gods.[1]

As these beliefs evolved, so did the Egyptians' obsession with death and eternal life. The torn-apart Osiris was put back together to attain immortality. Egyptians believed the pharaoh, the god-king, could be immortal only if his body was preserved for all time. They started building royal tombs, the largest of which is the Great Pyramid at Giza. They also developed the science of preserving the royal dead as mummies. These bodies would be preserved for thousands of years.

Kings and queens were buried with vast amounts of treasure, and the Egyptians wanted to protect the tombs from robbers. They sealed the tombs and put curses on the entrances to try to scare robbers away. For added insurance, at Giza, where they built the largest

CHAPTER 4

The Egyptian goddess Isis (left) was the mother of the falcon god Horus.

GODS, PHARAOHS, AND THE SPHINX

tombs in history, they built the greatest guardian the world had ever seen: something that could withstand the desert heat and wind, something that would protect against the evil in the world, something that symbolized the best of animal power and the best of human intelligence: the Great Sphinx.

How the Sphinx Was Built

The Great Sphinx was one of an awe-inspiring group of structures. They were huge and required a lot of leadership, money, engineering skills, and, of course, workers. They were all designed to glorify dead pharaohs and the sun god Re. They included the three Great Pyramids, the Pyramid Temple, the Sphinx, the Sphinx Temple, and the Valley Temple.

Scientists once thought the pyramids and the Sphinx were built by slaves. The idea came from Greek historian Herodotus, who wrote about an army of 100,000 slaves in Egypt. The problem is, Herodotus was born a couple of thousand years after the pyramids were built, so he didn't know for sure.[2]

Scientists have discovered that the Egyptians used skilled and paid craftsmen, along with paid workers, to build the pyramids. In 1985, American scientist Mark Lehner began excavating for the Giza Plateau Mapping Project. His team found animal remains at Giza. Most of the remains were from cattle, goats, and sheep. He calculated that if these animals had been slaughtered for food, there had been enough meat to feed at least 6,000 to 7,000 people. The workers were organized into teams of forty. They lived in buildings that were like military barracks. Some of these barracks had their own dining area, a bakery, and rows of beds.

An ancient worker cemetery was found just south of the Great Sphinx in 1990 when a tourist's horse stumbled over a sandy ruin. The cemetery, which contains remains from thousands of people who worked on the statue and the pyramids, dates from between 2575 and 2134 BCE. The workers were buried in mud-brick

CHAPTER 4

structures. Inscriptions and bones tell how physically demanding it was to build the pyramids and the Great Sphinx.

The Great Sphinx was built in a low area south of the great pyramid of Pharaoh Khufu in the northeastern area of the Valley Temple. That area was where workers had stored the huge stones to build the pyramids. Those stones were transported down the Nile from quarries in other parts of the kingdom.

Evidence suggests the Sphinx was built by Pharaoh Khafre. He was Khufu's son and ruled from 2520 to 2494 BCE. That time period of Egyptian history is known as the Old Kingdom (2575 to 2465 BCE).[3]

The Great Sphinx's body is 200 feet long—about the length of a city block—from paws to tail. It is 65 feet high, which is taller than a six-story building. Its face is 13 feet wide. Its eyes are 6 feet high. The Sphinx wears a pharaoh's nemes, which is a royal headdress. Part of the headdress—the ornament that looks like a sacred cobra—is missing.[4]

The Sphinx once had a 3-foot-long nose, but it is long gone. Soldiers under Napoleon were once blamed for blowing off the nose with a cannonball in the early 1800s while fighting battles in Egypt and the Middle East, but that is almost certainly another myth. Sketches of the Sphinx by Frederick Lewis Norden made in 1737 and published in 1755 showed the nose was missing then.

So what happened to the nose? Egyptian historian al-Maqrizi wrote in the fifteenth century CE that a fanatical Muslim named Muhammad Sa'im al-Dahr destroyed the nose. Sa'im al-Dahr said a group of Egyptian peasants made offerings to the Sphinx statue in 1378 for a good harvest. Apparently the peasants thought of the Sphinx as a magical god that could influence the Nile River's annual flooding. This angered Sa'im al-Dahr so much that he attacked the Sphinx and destroyed the nose. Another story is that the Sphinx was used by the Mamelukes—a group of people who ruled Egypt for more than 250 years, ending in 1517 CE—for target practice.

GODS, PHARAOHS, AND THE SPHINX

The Great Sphinx, shown guarding the pyramids at Giza, has been buried by sand, and then dug up, many times since it was built over 4,500 years ago.

CHAPTER 4

The Sphinx also once had a ceremonial beard, pieces of which are displayed at the British Museum in London and the Egyptian Museum in Cairo. Egyptologist Rainer Stadelmann said the beard was probably added when Egyptians were trying to show how the Sphinx represented the god Harmachis (Horus) sometime during the New Kingdom (1550 to 1070 BCE).[5] Although Egyptian men were clean-shaven, pharaohs wore false beards attached by straps to show their divinity.[6]

Between the Sphinx's front paws is a red granite tablet called the Dream Stele. On it is the story of Prince Thutmose and his dream about the Sphinx. Much of the writing has faded and can't be read. Here is a translation of what can be read:

> Behold me, O Thothmes, for I am the sun-god, the ruler of all peoples. Harmachis is my name and Ra, Khepera, and Tem. I am your father. You are my son. A lot of good things will happen if you listen to me. You shall have the land of Egypt. You shall rule for many years and be very rich and happy. . . . The sands of the desert are over me. Free me and do it quickly.[7]

Dream Stele of Thutmose IV

The story of the dream is probably not true. Egyptians usually feared dreams. They thought they came from the afterlife—like bad ghosts trying to harm the living.[8] The story was likely created for political purposes to give Thutmose an advantage over his older brothers. If the people believed he had a supernatural connection to the sun god, they would be more likely to make him pharaoh.

What Does It Mean?

Why was the Great Sphinx built? No record of its construction has ever been found. Ancient texts that mention it were written after it was built. What is known is that lions were considered guardian figures in ancient Egypt. The lion body represented strength, purification, and sun power. The bull-like neck represented spiritual purity. The human head represented god-inspired intelligence, the knowledge of good and evil, and the greatest evolution of the body.

Protective sphinxes were usually carved lying down, like the Great Sphinx, although some were shown trampling Egypt's enemies. One theory is that the Great Sphinx was built to guard the Giza Plateau. It was the symbol of the sun god and faces the rising sun, so it would have protected the dead in the tombs around it.

German Egyptologist Herbert Ricke claimed the Sphinx was part of a solar cult (a group that worshiped the sun) and was built during the Fourth Dynasty (around 2500 BCE) as part of the image of Hor-Em-Akhet, or "Horus of the Horizon"—the Egyptian sun god.[9]

Take a good look at the Great Sphinx and you'll notice that the head is too small for its body. This is unusual because the Egyptians usually designed and built things in proportion.[10] Some scientists believe the head was changed in ancient times. It might once have shown the head of an animal and then was carved again into a human face. Some believe the original head was that of the god Anubis, which is represented by a dog or a jackal.[11]

Other scientists disagree. They say that because this was one of the first Egyptian sphinxes to be built, the rules of proportion might not have been used yet.[12] Another possibility is that it was built that way so that it looked its best when viewed from close up. Maybe there wasn't enough good rock to make a larger head. Or maybe a crack at the rear of the Sphinx forced the builders to make a longer body rather than a shorter one. The bottom line is we'll never know for sure—unless records are someday discovered.

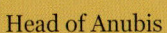

Head of Anubis

An ancient bust of Khafre, the pharaoh whose image is believed to be the carved head of the Great Sphinx. Note the headdress (nemes) and the false beard.

THE SPHINX

CHAPTER 5
Why a Sphinx?

Historians believe the head of the Great Sphinx was carved in the image of Pharaoh Khafre. Why not just make a big statue of him rather than that of a mythical creature? That's how we build memorials today. For instance, you don't see a half human, half animal statue at the Lincoln Memorial. You see a huge sculpture of a seated Abraham Lincoln.

Part of the reason is that pharaohs were supposed to be gods. Mixing human and animal forms showcased a supernatural connection, because gods were often represented through animals. The god Horus was shown as a falcon, Khnum as a ram, Thoth as an ibis, Hathar as a cow, and Sobek as a crocodile.[1]

Early Egyptians were in awe of the animals around them. Many of those animals were bigger and stronger and faster than humans. An unarmed man going against, say, a lion, was in for trouble. Over time, as people developed better weapons and hunting strategies, they got the upper hand. Many scholars think hybrid creatures such as the Sphinx symbolize man's control over nature's beasts. The Sphinx shows that human intelligence is greater than animal power. It also shows the best of both worlds. What could be better than having the intellect of a human and the strength of a lion?[2]

In sphinx artwork, the body indicates the god and the head shows the person's identity. Having a headdress (nemes) shows royalty. Putting it all together links the pharaoh with humans and gods. The lion was a symbol for the sun and royalty as well as a guardian.

Chapter 5

Other Mesopotamian (Middle Eastern) cultures mixed species as well. The griffin had the head of an eagle and the body of a lion. They also showed leopards with snakelike necks.

The Sphinx wasn't called the Sphinx in Egyptian times. Over the years it was known as Horem-Akhet (Horus in the Horizon) and Ra-horakhty (Ra of Two Horizons), although maybe the most popular name was Harmachis (Horus of the Two Horizons).

In later Egyptian times, sphinxes were sometimes referred to with the phrase *shesep ankh Atum* (living image of Atum). Atum was an Egyptian creator god who represented the setting sun. There is a link in Egyptian mythology between Atum and a lion, which was considered the first creature to emerge from creation.

This view of the Great Sphinx shows the head is small in relation to the lion body. The Dream Stele is between its paws, and the Great Pyramid of Khufu is in the background.

WHY A SPHINX?

Near the Great Sphinx is the Sphinx Temple, which appears to have been built in connection to the solar cycle. Its roof is supported by 24 columns, which are thought to represent the 24 hours in a day. People who are at the Sphinx during the summer solstice can watch the sun set between the pyramids of Khufu and Khafre. (The summer solstice is when the sun is most overhead, giving the longest day of the year. In the northern hemisphere, it happens in late June.) That view is very much like the hieroglyph for "horizon," which is a drawing of the sun setting between two mountains.[3]

The body of the Sphinx is made of soft sandstone. Although it is easy to work with, it erodes fairly quickly in Egypt's harsh desert. The Sphinx was protected because it was buried in sand up to its neck for most of its existence. It has been completely free of sand for the last hundred years, so it is constantly exposed to pollution from nearby Cairo as well as wind and the sun. Egyptian officials are trying to preserve it. Early attempts failed, but in the 1980s officials began a careful restoration. Over six years they added more than 2,000 limestone blocks to the body. Preserving chemicals were injected into the stone, but that proved disastrous when the new stone flaked off along with the original stone.

Then officials tried using mortar and workers who were not trained in restoration. The result proved disastrous once again. The left shoulder crumbled and limestone blocks fell off.

The next plan involved draining water away from the ground near the Sphinx because officials thought underground seepage was damaging the rock. Officials also repaired the damaged shoulder. The statue has survived for nearly 5,000 years. Egyptian officials hope it will last at least another 5,000 years.

Even in ancient Greek and Roman times, the Great Sphinx and the Great Pyramids were big tourist draws. Scientists have found old Greek and Roman graffiti there from those times. Egypt was once closed to visitors from other countries, but that changed under leaders in the Ptolemy family. They were of Greek origin and they

Chapter 5

Egyptians used the Great Sphinx's temple to worship the power of the sun.

allowed outside visitors to see the great sites, including the monuments and temples at Giza. Why? For the money. The last of the fifteen Ptolemy rulers were Queen Cleopatra and her son Ptolemy XV. The Romans took control of Egypt after defeating Cleopatra and Roman General Mark Antony at the Battle of Actium in 30 BCE. The Romans also allowed visitors into Egypt, and thousands came to explore Giza. They brought back new tales and mythologies to explain the existence of the Great Sphinx.[4]

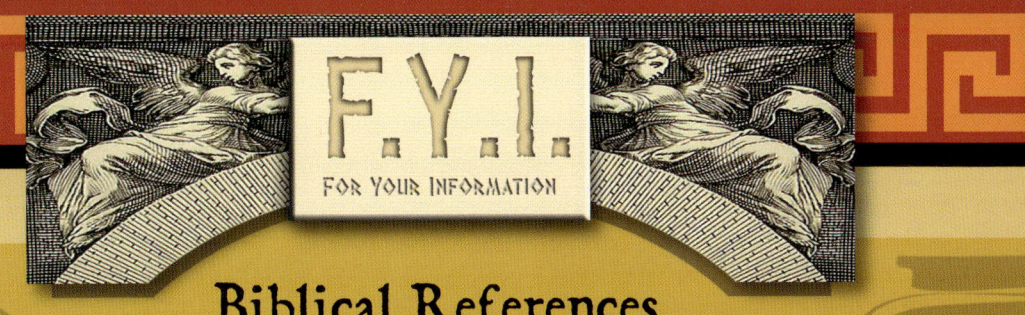

Biblical References

Does the Bible mention sphinxes? Perhaps. In the Book of Revelation, John writes that he saw a door in heaven open and God sitting on his throne. There was a sea of glass in front of the throne, and around the throne were four beasts. Here is how John described them:

> The first creature resembled a lion, and the second was like a calf, and the third had a face like that of a human being and the fourth looked like an eagle in flight. The four living creatures, each of them with six wings, were covered with eyes inside and out; day and night they do not stop exclaiming: Holy, holy, holy, is the Lord God Almighty, who was, and who is to come.[5]

These beasts around God's throne were like guardians, just as the Great Sphinx was believed to guard the pyramids.

There's another possible sphinx-like image from the prophet Ezekiel. Ezekiel writes that a huge cloud of flashing fire appeared to him in a vision. He saw four creatures in the cloud that looked like men, but weren't human. Each creature had four faces and wings. Each also had the feet of a calf. He writes: "Their faces were like this: each of the four had the face of a man, but on the right side was the face of a lion, and on the left side the face of an ox, and finally each had the face of an eagle."[6]

The prophet Ezekiel wrote long before John wrote the Book of Revelation. His creatures also show the combination of animal and human, plus the guardian role, found within the Sphinx legend.

This doesn't mean Ezekiel actually saw a sphinx, but it does show how images in the writings of one culture often appear in another.

Ezekiel by Raphael

CHAPTER NOTES

Chapter 1. Riddle Me This
1. Sophocles, *Oedipus the King*, translated by Bernard Knox (New York: Simon and Schuster Publishing, 2005), pp. 5–83.
2. Sophocles, *Three Theban Plays*, translated by Peter Constantine (New York: Barnes & Noble Books, 2007), pp. 5–71.

Chapter 2. Oedipus Finds the Truth
1. Sophocles, *Oedipus the King*, translated by Bernard Knox (New York: Simon and Schuster Publishing, 2005), pp. 5–83.
2. David P. Silverman, *Ancient Egypt* (New York: Oxford University Press-Duncan Baird Publishers, 1997), pp. 186–187.
3. *The Sphinx, Egypt*, http://www.ancient-wisdom.co.uk/egyptsphinx.htm

Chapter 3. From Prince to Pharaoh
1. *Ancient Egypt—The Mythology*: "The Prince and the Sphinx," http://www.egyptianmyths.net/mythsphinx.htm
2. Evan Hadingham, "Uncovering Secrets of the Sphinx," *Smithsonian*, February 2010, pp. 32–41.
3. David P. Silverman, *Ancient Egypt* (New York: Oxford University Press-Duncan Baird Publishers, 1997), p. 186.
4. Editors of Time-Life Books, *The Age of God-Kings* (Richmond, Va.: Time-Life Books, 1987), pp. 57–58.
5. *The Gods of Ancient Egypt*, "Horus," http://www.touregypt.net/godsofegypt/horus.htm

Chapter 4. Gods, Pharaohs, and the Sphinx
1. Editors of Time-Life Books, *The Age of God-Kings* (Richmond, Va.: Time-Life Books, 1987), pp. 55–57.
2. Alexander Stille, "35 Who Made a Difference: Mark Lehner," *Smithsonian*, November 1, 2005, http://www.smithsonianmag.com/people-places/lehner.html
3. Evan Hadingham, "Uncovering Secrets of the Sphinx," *Smithsonian*, February 2010, p. 34.
4. *Tour Egypt*: "The Great Sphinx" http://interoz.com/egypt/sphinx.htm
5. Zawi Hawass, "The Great Sphinx," http://www.drhawass.com/blog/story-sphinx
6. Way2Egypt: "Egyptian Sphinx," http://www.way2egypt.com/sphinx.html
7. Jacques Kinnaer, *The Ancient Egypt Site*, http://www.ancient-egypt.org/index.html
8. Gary Glassman, *NOVA*: "Interview of Kasia Szpakowska, Conducted March 22, 2009," edited by Susan K. Lewis, http://www.pbs.org/wgbh/nova/ancient/sphinx-stela.html

CHAPTER NOTES

9. David P. Silverman, *Ancient Egypt* (New York: Oxford University Press-Duncan Baird Publishers, 1997), p. 186.
10. Robert Temple with Olivia Temple, *The Sphinx Mystery—The Forgotten Origins of the Sanctuary of Anubis* (Rochester, VT: Inner Traditions, 2009), p. 6.
11. Ibid., p. 202.
12. Ibid.

Chapter 5. Why a Sphinx?

1. Allen Winston, "The Meaning of the Great Sphinx of Giza," *Tour Egypt*, http://www.touregypt.net/featurestories/sphinx4.htm
2. Ibid.
3. Evan Hadingham, "Uncovering Secrets of the Sphinx," *Smithsonian*, February 2010, pp. 32–41.
4. Robert Temple with Olivia Temple, *The Sphinx Mystery—The Forgotten Origins of the Sanctuary of Anubis* (Rochester, VT: Inner Traditions, 2009), p. 10.
5. *The New American Bible*, Book of Revelation, 4:1-2, 4:6, 4:7-8.
6. *The New American Bible*, Book of Ezekiel, 1:4–7, 10.

FURTHER READING

Books

Fletcher, Joann. *Exploring The Life, Myth, and Art of Ancient Egypt*. New York: Rosen Publishing Group, 2009.

Kramer, Ann. *Egyptian Myth: A Treasury of Legends, Art and History*. Armonk, N.Y.: Sharpe Focus, 2007.

Mortensen, Lori. *Sphinx*. San Diego: Kidhaven Press, 2007.

Schomp, Virginia. *The Ancient Egyptians*. Salt Lake City: Benchmark Books, 2007.

Strachan, Bruce. *Ancient Egypt: A First Look at People of the Nile*. New York: Henry Holt and Co., 2008.

Works Consulted

Colavito, Jason. "Who Built the Sphinx?" http://jcolavito.tripod.com/lostcivilizations/id17.html

Editors of Time-Life Books. *The Age of God-Kings*. Richmond, Va.: Time-Life Books, 1987.

Editors of Time-Life Books. *Psychic Powers*. Richmond, Va.: Time-Life Books, 1987.

Grant, Michael. *Myths of the Greeks and Romans*. New York: Meridian, Penguin Group, 1995.

Hadingham, Evan. "Uncovering Secrets of the Sphinx." *Smithsonian*, February 2010, pp. 32–41.

FURTHER READING

Hamilton, Edith. *Mythology*. New York: Little, Brown & Co., 1942.

Hawass, Dr. Zawi, and Mark Lehner. "The Sphinx, Who Built It and Why." *Archaeology Magazine*, September–October 1994.

Reid, Robin T. "Digging Up Egypt's Treasures—The Ten Most Significant Discoveries in the Past 20 Years." *Smithsonian Magazine*, November 5, 2007. http://www.smithsonianmag.com/history-archaeology/egypt-topten.html

Robinson, Charles Alexander Jr. *Sophocles, the Theban Saga*. New York: Franklin Watts Inc., 1966. *Oedipus the King*, translated by Clarence W. Mendell.

Seleen, Dr. Ramses. *Egyptian Book of the Dead*. New York: Sterling Publishing Co., 2001.

Silverman, David P. *Ancient Egypt*. New York: Oxford University Press-Duncan Baird Publishers, 1997.

Sophocles. *Oedipus the King*. Translated by Bernard Knox. New York: Simon and Schuster Publishing, 2005.

———. *Three Theban Plays*. Translated by Peter Constantine. New York: Barnes & Noble Books, 2007.

Spence, Lewis. *Ancient Egyptian Myths and Legends*. New York: Barnes and Noble Inc, 2005. Originally published in 1915.

Sunfellow, David. "The Great Pyramid and the Sphinx, a Summary of Current Archeological, Geological and Psychic Controversies," *New Heaven, New Earth*, November 25, 1994. http://www.nhne.com/specialreports/srpyramid.html

Temple, Robert, with Olivia Temple. *The Sphinx Mystery—The Forgotten Origins of the Sanctuary of Anubis*. Rochester, VT: Inner Traditions.

Wilkinson, Richard H. *The Complete Gods and Goddesses of Ancient Egypt*. London: Thames & Hudson, 2003.

On the Internet

Ancient Egypt—The Mythology: "The Prince and the Sphinx"
http://www.egyptianmyths.net/mythsphinx.htm

Ancient Egyptian Culture: The Sphinx
http://www.mnsu.edu/emuseum/prehistory/egypt/archaeology/weirdtheories/sphinx.html

Great Sphinx
http://interoz.com/egypt/sphinx.htm

The Great Sphinx of Giza
http://www.touregypt.net/featurestories/sphinx1.htm

"The Mystery of the Sphinx"
http://www.altarcheologie.nl/egypt/The%20Mystery%20of%20the%20Sphinx.htm

Who Built the Sphinx?
http://jcolavito.tripod.com/lostcivilizations/id17.html

World Mythology—Egyptian Mythology
http://library.thinkquest.org/03oct/01263/Egyptian.htm

GLOSSARY

artifact (AR-tih-fakt)—An object made or shaped by humans.

castrate (KAS-trayt)—To remove the reproductive organs.

dynasty (DY-nus-tee)—A succession of rulers who are members of the same family.

Egyptologist (ee-jip-TAH-luh-jist)—Someone who studies the culture and treasures of ancient Egypt.

exile (EK-zyl)—To be forced out of one's country.

graffiti (gruh-FEE-tee)—Drawings or words that deface walls or other property.

hieroglyphs (HY-roh-glifs)—Ancient Egyptian writing that used symbols rather than letters.

hybrid (HY-brid)—A cross between two very different things, such as offspring of two animals or species. In mythology, hybrids are usually part human and part animal, god, or goddess.

immortality (ih-mor-TAL-ih-tee)—Ability to live forever. In mythology, gods and goddesses have this gift.

ligament (LIG-uh-munt)—One of the ropy tissues that connect the bones in the body.

nymph (NIMF)—A female spirit in Greek and Roman mythology.

oracle (OR-uh-kul)—A person who tells the future.

pharaoh (FAA-roh)—An Egyptian king.

sphinx (SFINKS)—A mythical creature with the body of a lion and head of a human. Greek sphinxes had heads of women and wings. Egyptian sphinxes had heads of men and did not have wings.

stele (STEEL-ee)—A stone slab that tells a story, usually found on large monuments or buildings.

variations (vayr-ee-AY-shunz)—Differences.

venomous (VEH-nuh-mus)—Full of poison.

PHOTO CREDITS: Cover, pp. 1, 13—Joe Rasemas; pp. 6, 22, 24, 28, 30, 32, 35, 36, 38, 40, 42—CreativeCommons; p. 8—Rembrandt Harmenszoon van Rijn; p. 11—Gustave Moreau; p. 14—Jean-Auguste-Dominique Ingres; pp. 17, 27—Carly Peterson; p. 20—Fulchran-Jean Harriet; p. 43—Raffaello Sanzio da Urbino. Every effort has been made to locate all copyright holders of material used in this book. If any errors or omissions have occurred, corrections will be made in future editions of this book.

INDEX

Amenhotep II 22, 23, 28
Amun 21
Antigone 20
Anubis 37
Apollo 16
Atum 40
Battle of Actium 42
Cairo 21, 23, 36, 41
Cerberus 13
Chimaera, the 13
Cleopatra 42
Corinth 7, 9, 10, 15, 18
Creon 18, 19, 20
Crete 21
Delphi 9, 16, 18
Dream Stele 28, 36, 40
Echidna 13
Egypt 17, 20, 21, 23, 26, 27, 28, 29, 30, 31, 33, 34, 36, 37, 39, 40, 41, 42
Geb 29
Giza 21, 25, 27, 31, 33, 35, 37, 42
Great Pyramids 23, 25, 31, 33, 35, 41
Greece 17, 20, 21
Harmachis 25, 29, 36
Hathar 39
Headdress (nemes) 34, 38, 39
Hera (Juno) 7, 8, 9, 10, 14
Herodotus 33
Hieroglyphs 30, 41
Horus 28, 29, 32, 36, 37, 39, 40
Isis 22, 29, 32
Jocasta 14, 15–16, 18, 19
Khafre (Chephren) 25, 34, 38, 39, 41
Khnum 39
Khufu (Cheops) 25, 34, 40, 41
Laius 15, 16, 18
Lehner, Mark 33
Memphis 27, 31
Menes 31
Menkaure (Mykerinos) 25
Merope 9, 15, 18
Mesopotamia (Middle East) 21, 34, 40
Muses 9, 12
Napoleon 34
Nemean Lion 13
Nile River 21, 23, 24, 25, 29, 34
Oedipus 9–10, 11, 12, 14, 15–16, 18–20
Oracle at Delphi 9, 16, 18
Osiris 29, 30, 31
Pharaoh 23, 25, 26, 28, 29, 31, 33, 34, 36, 38, 39
Polybus 9, 15, 18
Ptolemy 41, 42
Re (Ra) 23, 28, 33, 36, 40
Seth 29
Sicily 13
Sobek 39
Sphinx, Egyptian
   construction 33–34, 36, 37
   description 20, 21, 25, 29, 36, 37
   myth 23–26, 28, 42
   nose 34
   origin 21, 31, 33
   preservation 41
   symbolism 37, 39
Sphinx, Greek
   description 6, 10, 21
   heritage 13
   myth 7, 9–10, 11, 12, 17, 20
   origin 20
   riddle 10, 11, 12, 14, 19
Sphinx Temple 33, 41, 42
Summer solstice 41
Teiresias 18
Thebes (Egypt) 27
Thebes (Greece) 9, 10, 12, 17, 18, 19, 20, 27
Thoth 39
Thutmose IV 22, 23–26, 28, 29, 36
Typhon 13
Underworld 19, 29
Zeus 12, 13, 16, 21

398.22 D   HKASX
DiPrimio, Pete.
The sphinx /

KASHMERE GARDENS
02/11